Victorian Life

Homes

Nicola Barber

WAYLAND

First published in 2008
by Wayland

Copyright © Wayland 2008

Wayland
338 Euston Road
London NW1 3BH

Wayland Australia
Level 17/207 Kent Street
Sydney, NSW 2000

Editor: Katie Powell
Designer: Jane Hawkins
Concept design: Paul Cherrill

British Library Cataloguing in Publication Data

Barber, Nicola
   Homes. - (Victorian life)
   1. Dwellings - Great Britain - History - 19th century -
   Juvenile literature 2. Great Britain - Social life and
   customs - 19th century - Juvenile literature
   I. Title
   643.1'0941'09034
ISBN 978 0 7502 5367 3

Picture acknowledgements: Bettmann/Corbis: 22 Mark
Boulton/Alamy: 12 Bridgeman Art Library/J. Atkinson
Grimshaw/Getty Images: 3, 13 Bridgeman Art Library/
English School/Getty Images: 21 Mary Evans Picture
Library: COVER (main image) 6, 9, 10, 19B, 20, 23, 24,
26 Johnny Greig/Alamy: 8 Bert Hardy/Hulton Archive/
Getty Images: 17T Brian Harrison/Kudos; Elizabeth
Whiting & Assocs./Corbis: 27 Hulton Archive/Getty
Images: 25 Mike Kipling Photography: 11 Jeff Morgan
heritage/Alamy: 15 Travelshots.com/Alamy: 14 Wayland
Archive: 4, 5, 16, 17B, 18, 19T, 28 World History Archive/
TopFoto.co.uk: 7
With thanks to www.victorianlondon.org for the
quote on p9

Printed in China

Wayland is a division of Hachette Children's Books,
an Hachette Livre UK company, www.hachettelivre.co.uk

Contents

Words in **bold** can be found
in the glossary.

Victorian change

The long **reign** of Queen Victoria was a time of huge change in Britain. When Victoria came to the throne in 1837, most people lived in the countryside and the development of the railways had only just begun.

A time of change

By the time Queen Victoria died in 1901, Britain's population had more than doubled and roughly three-quarters of these people lived in towns and cities. The railway network connected all parts of Britain and the first motor cars had been seen on the roads.

The Industrial Revolution

The driving force behind the change was the **Industrial Revolution**. This began in the late 1700s, with the invention of machines that could perform jobs previously done by hand, and was well under way when Queen Victoria came to the throne. For example, the invention of machines that could spin and weave cloth quickly transformed the textile industry. By the 1780s, there were more than 120 textile mills in Britain.

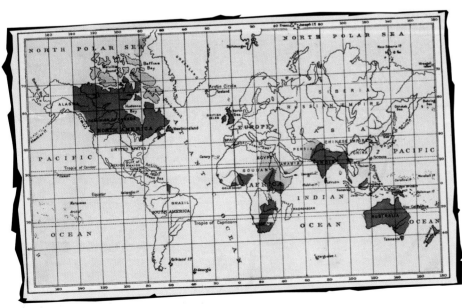

This map, dating from the 1880s, shows the extent of the **British Empire** at that time (in red).

The other main factors in the Industrial Revolution were the development of steam engines to power the new machinery, and a good supply of coal to fuel these engines. Coal was also used in the production of iron, vital for the construction of machines and tools.

The transport revolution

In 1837, Queen Victoria inherited a vast empire that stretched across the world. The **colonies** of this empire provided not only the **raw materials** needed to supply Britain's new factories and mills, but also people to buy the goods that were made. Both the raw materials and the finished goods had to be transported over long distances, and so the Industrial Revolution also sparked off a revolution in transport.

At first, waterways were used to carry goods. Between the 1780s and the 1830s, many kilometres of canals were dug across Britain. Roads were also improved and in the 1830s, the construction of the railways began.

Queen Victoria, 1819–1901

Victoria was only 18 years old when she became the Queen of the United Kingdom in 1837. Her reign, which lasted nearly 64 years, was longer than that of any other British monarch. During the Victorian era Britain became a global power thanks to its industrial progress, and to its vast overseas empire. Some years after India became part of the British Empire, in 1876, Victoria also became Empress of India.

⇧ Raw materials and finished goods from a ceramics factory called Etruria Works were transported along the Trent and Mersey Canal which ran alongside the factory.

Victorian homes

The Industrial Revolution changed many aspects of life in Britain, including how people built their houses and the materials that were used to build them. In most towns and cities in Britain today you can find examples of Victorian homes.

⬆ Many people in London and other British towns and cities live in Victorian houses today.

Building materials

In previous centuries, people mostly used local materials for their homes, because transporting heavy building materials over long distances was difficult and expensive. But the development of the railways and improvements to roads during the Victorian era meant that the transport of goods from one place to another became much easier.

New **manufacturing** processes also meant that bricks could be made more cheaply and efficiently than ever before. **Mass-produced** bricks made in factories were regular in shape and reliable in quality, and they were used across the country to build all sorts of buildings from factories to homes.

Big and small

Many wealthy people built grand country houses (see pages 14–15) while the middle classes lived in comfortable houses or in 'villas' (see pages 12–13). Houses for workers were often built in long rows, called **terraces** (see pages 10–11). Many of these houses shared the same **architectural** features. See how many you can spot in your neighbourhood:

1. Sash windows
2. Bay windows
3. Name and date plaques
4. Decorative brickwork
5. Finials
6. Iron railings
7. Bargeboards

⬆ This Victorian semi-detached house has many typical decorative features.

The growth of cities

The Industrial Revolution meant thousands of people moved from their homes in the countryside to the towns and cities. People could find better-paid and more regular work in the new mills and factories there.

Expanding towns

Towns and cities grew rapidly during the Victorian era, as new houses were built for the workers. The owners of the mills and factories wanted people to live close to their work, so that they could walk to and fro, and hear the hooter that sounded the start and end of the working day.

Back-to-backs

These new houses were usually built quickly and cheaply. In the north of England, many houses were built 'back-to-back'. These were long, double rows of houses, called terraces, each one sharing its side and back walls with the house next door. As there was only one outside wall for windows, these houses were often dark. In Scotland, many people lived in blocks of flats called **tenements**.

⬆ This engraving by Gustav Doré shows back-to-back housing in London, 1870.

Written at the time

The terrible conditions in which many workers lived in the town of Bradford are described in an article in *The Bradford Observer* newspaper, on 16 October, 1845:

'In a portion of this town [Bradford] called The Leys, there are scores of wretched hovels, unfurnished and unventilated, damp, filthy in the extreme and surrounded by stagnant pools of human excrement and every thing offensive and disgusting to "sight and smell". No sewers, no drainage, no ventilation. Nothing to be seen but squalid wretchedness on every side ...'

Model houses

Some factory owners wanted their workers to live in better conditions. In 1850, a mill-owner called Titus Salt (1803–1876) announced plans to build a model community at Saltaire near Bradford to house his 3,500 workers. He built decent houses, as well as a school, library, hospital, church and shops. In 1879, George and Richard Cadbury started work on the Bournville estate in Birmingham for the workers in their chocolate factory. You can still visit Saltaire and Bournville today.

⬆ Saltaire took its name from its founder Titus Salt and the river next to which it was built, the River Aire. Today it is a World Heritage Site.

Life in the suburbs

Victorian cities were dirty, smelly and noisy. While poor workers had little choice about living close to the factories and mills, many of those who could afford it chose to move further out of the cities into the **suburbs**.

Peace and quiet

In the suburbs people hoped to find cleaner air and more peaceful streets. The growth of the suburbs was made possible by the development of transport links between the suburbs and cities. Every working day, Victorian middle class men travelled by railway, **tram** or horse-drawn buses from their homes to their jobs.

Terraces and villas

Houses in the suburbs varied from long terraces of small houses to rather grander detached or semi-detached 'villas'. But while many suburban houses had decorative features on the outside such as bay windows and fancy chimney pots, inside they were often cheaply built and damp.

This semi-detached villa is built in typical Victorian style. How many of the features listed on page 9 can you spot?

Most terraced houses had no bathroom, although houses built after 1875 had to have a toilet by law. Inside, there was a parlour at the front, used only on Sundays or to receive guests, and a kitchen at the back. Upstairs were two or three bedrooms. Villas for wealthier people had larger rooms, often with a kitchen in the basement and attic rooms in the roof where the servants lived.

Written at the time

In his comic novel, *The Diary of a Nobody*, published in 1892, George Grossmith pokes fun at a middle-class clerk, Charles Pooter, and his family:

'My dear wife Carrie and I have just been a week in our new house, "The Laurels", Brickfield Terrace, Holloway — a nice six-roomed residence, not counting the basement, with a front breakfast-parlour. We have a little front garden; and there is a flight of ten steps up to the front door ... We have a nice little back garden which runs down to the railway. We were rather afraid of the noise of the trains at first, but the landlord said we should not notice them after a bit, and took 2 pounds off the rent.'

⬅ This large Victorian house has a big entrance hall, decorated with expensive furniture.

Stately homes

While the poor endured horribly cramped living conditions, often with many people living in one room, the wealthiest families lived in spacious and luxurious homes with servants to attend to their every need.

Wealth and luxury

The Industrial Revolution brought vast wealth to some landowners and industrialists, and many of them spent huge amounts on lavish country homes. The Tyneside industrialist Lord Armstrong made his fortune with a highly successful manufacturing business. He built Cragside in Northumberland as his country home, and in the 1870s, it became the first house in the world to be lit by electricity. In 1863, another wealthy businessman, William Gibbs, built Tyntesfield in North Somerset. This highly decorated house cost £70,000 to build – the equivalent of more than £4 million today.

Cragside in Northumberland is now owned by the National Trust. A visit offers a fascinating insight into how wealthy Victorians ran their homes.

The servants' bells at Tyntesfield in North Somerset. Each bell was labelled so that the servants knew in which room they were needed when it rang.

Backwell Room. · Belmont Room · Portbury Room · Billiard Room · Lou... Ro...

Ante Room · His Lordship's Dressing Room. · Oak Room · Bath Room

Cragside and Tyntesfield

Both Cragside and Tyntesfield were very large houses – Tyntesfield had a total of 43 bedrooms! Such grand houses had rooms for different times of day and functions, for example a morning room, a library, a drawing room, a billiards room and a smoking room. In many stately homes, up to 40 servants were employed. These included a **butler**, cooks, a housekeeper, **footmen**, kitchen maids, housemaids, lady's maids, laundry maids, gardeners, stable hands, gamekeepers and coachmen.

A day in the life of...

...a housemaid who worked under the supervision of the housekeeper. Her work was often back-breaking and exhausting:

'My day starts at 6 o'clock in the morning when I wake up in my small room at the top of the house. It's cold – there's no fire up here – and I quickly wash in a bowl of cold water and dress. My first job is to make tea for the housekeeper and lady's maid. Then I start about the real business of the day, fetching hot water for the Master and Mistress and emptying the chamber pots, making the beds and cleaning the bedrooms. I clear the ashes out of the fireplaces, and clean and polish the grates. I brush the carpets and beat the rugs to get rid of the dirt. Then the candlesticks must be polished ready for dinner. My day usually ends at around 10.30 in the evening – or later if the housekeeper has any other jobs for me.'

Homes for the poor

Victorian Britain was the richest and most powerful country in the world, yet for the poorest people life was extremely hard. Most worked long hours, often in horrible conditions, for little pay.

Living conditions

Many families could afford no more than one room in a damp and draughty house where everyone had to live and sleep together. People collected water from the nearest supply, and up to 30 families frequently relied on just one tap for their water.

Life in the countryside

For the poor, life in the countryside was just as tough as in the cities. The Industrial Revolution saw small-scale **cottage industries**, such as lace-making or weaving and spinning, killed off by the arrival of the mills and factories. These industries had once provided an income for those in rural areas but many people were forced to leave the countryside to find work in the towns and cities.

 Many poor country people were forced to leave their villages to look for work in the towns.

Dr Barnardo, 1845–1905

Thomas Barnardo was born in Dublin and arrived in London in 1866 to train as a doctor. He was appalled by the poverty he saw around him, particularly by the thousands of homeless children. In 1870 he opened a home for homeless and penniless boys in Stepney, and in 1876 the Girls' Village Home in Barkingside. By the time of his death in 1905, nearly 60,000 children had been rescued and helped to find better lives.

This scene from the 1948 film *Oliver Twist* shows a woman seeking refuge at a workhouse.

The workhouse punishment book was used to record offences committed by the inmates.

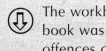

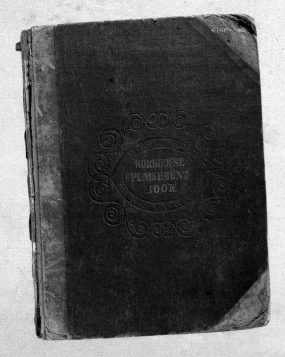

The workhouse

For those who were too old or sick to work, and who did not have a home, the only alternative was the **workhouse**. Workhouses were deliberately designed to be unpleasant places to live in order to discourage the 'undeserving poor'. Men, women and children were housed separately, so families were split up when they entered a workhouse. The food was basic, and those who were able were required to do such jobs as crushing bones for fertilizer, breaking stones for road mending, or domestic tasks such as cleaning and washing.

Light and heat

Victorian homes were heated with open fires. The rich could afford a fireplace in every room and kitchens had large iron ranges for cooking.

Large ranges such as this one were found in the homes of the wealthy.

Fires and ranges

The coal fire inside a kitchen range was kept burning to produce hot water as well as heat an oven and hobs for cooking. Everyday, fires and ranges had to be cleaned thoroughly. In cities, the soot and smoke from millions of coal fires and factories created thick **smogs** and covered everything in a layer of dust. From the 1870s onwards, hot water pipes were installed into the homes of some wealthier people to take water upstairs.

At night

At bedtime, beds were warmed either with stone hot water bottles filled with boiling water, or by bags of sand that were heated over the kitchen range. To light rooms, candles or oil lamps were used. Oil lamps gave out a dim glow and had to be cleaned regularly to prevent them from becoming clogged and dirty.

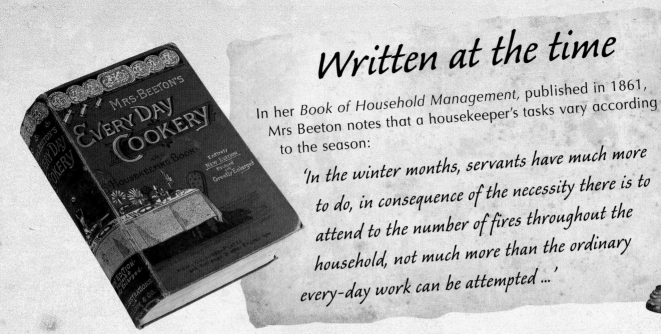

In her *Book of Household Management*, published in 1861, Mrs Beeton notes that a housekeeper's tasks vary according to the season:

'In the winter months, servants have much more to do, in consequence of the necessity there is to attend to the number of fires throughout the household, not much more than the ordinary every-day work can be attempted ...'

From the 1870s onwards, gaslights became more common in houses. The gas was pumped into houses through pipes. Gas light was much brighter than the light from oil lamps.

Electric light

In 1879, a British inventor called Joseph Swan demonstrated the first practical light bulb at a lecture in Newcastle. Another inventor, the American Thomas Edison, had also been working on the light bulb and in 1883, the two men established the Edison & Swan United Electric Light Company. However, by the end of the Victorian era electric light still remained a novelty, and most people continued to light their homes with candles, oil lamps and gaslights.

This advert for oil lamps dated 1888, shows that these lamps remained popular throughout the Victorian period.

Bathrooms and toilets

At the Great Exhibition of 1851, one of the attractions was the installation of flushing toilets for public use. Over 827,000 people paid to use these toilets and they eventually became a common feature in the home.

Keeping clean

Most early Victorian houses, however, had no bathroom or toilet. For those who could afford servants, hot water for washing was brought up every morning by a maid and a chamber pot, kept beneath the bed for night time use, was cleaned. People bathed in their bedrooms in hip baths, so-called because the water came up to their hips.

Public bath houses

For people in poorer homes, keeping clean was a struggle. Families often shared one water pump and one **privy** with many others. In 1846, parliament passed an Act to allow local parishes to build public baths and laundries. For a small fee, people could have a hot bath and wash their clothes.

This advertisement for Pears' soap dates from the 1890s and shows a child about to get into a hip bath.

A smelly problem

Bathrooms and indoor toilets were common in wealthy and middle-class homes from the 1870s onwards. But the disposal of **sewage** was a problem. Most sewage emptied into ditches or **cesspits** which were drained into the nearest river. Outbreaks of **cholera**, a disease that is spread through dirty, infected water, killed thousands of people in 1848–1849 and 1853–1854.

In London, sewage in the River Thames smelled so bad that the summer of 1858 became known as the 'Great Stink'. Wealthy residents left the city, or hung perfumed sheets up in their homes to mask the smell. In the following year, work started on an underground system of tunnels to carry London's sewage away from the city to the Thames estuary. By 1865 London had 2,100 kilometres of sewers.

⬆ Elaborate baths and showers became very popular amongst well-off Victorians. This model dates from the 1890s.

Edwin Chadwick, 1800–1890

Edwin Chadwick devoted much of his life to campaigning for improvements in hygiene and public health. In 1842, he published 'An inquiry into the Sanitary Conditions of the Labouring Population of Great Britain,' in which he argued that improving conditions for the lower classes would help to save public money. In this inquiry, he recommended that the most important action was 'the removal of all refuse of habitations, streets, and roads, and the improvement of the supplies of water.' He was knighted in 1889, becoming Sir Edwin Chadwick.

Running a household

One reason for the huge numbers of servants employed during the Victorian era was that keeping a home clean and warm, and a large family fed and healthy, was extremely hard work. Most jobs were done by hand rather than by machine.

This advertisement for a combined washer and wringer dates from the 1870s. Such devices were supposed to help the mistress of the house and her servants with the laborious task of washing.

Wash day

Washing was a back-breaking and time-consuming task. In wealthy homes, it was done by the laundry maids. Saturdays and Sundays were spent sorting the laundry, treating stains and soaking the laundry to prepare it for washing.

On Monday the maids got up extra early to light a fire in the furnace that heated the water boiler. The hot water was poured into huge tubs, where the dirty linen was washed by hand, then rinsed several times and wrung-out by hand, before being hung out to dry. By Thursday and Friday, the dry items were pressed either by putting them through a **mangle** – two heavy rollers turned by a handle – or by ironing with an iron heated on the range.

Household gadgets

Towards the end of the era, new hand-operated washers began to appear. Many of these had wringers which helped to squeeze water out of the washing. Other gadgets to appear in Victorian homes included hand-operated carpet sweepers and flushing toilets (see pages 20–21).
In 1879, the first telephone exchange opened in London and telephones were installed into the homes of a few wealthy people.

A day in the life of...

...the cook who was in charge of the kitchen in a wealthy home. She also had maids to help her:

'My day starts at 6 in the morning. The kitchen maids light the fires in the kitchen, and the scullery maids clean the kitchen floors and tables. Meanwhile I must bake the dough made last night for the breakfast rolls. After breakfast I meet with my Mistress to discuss the menus for the day. Then the morning is taken up with preparing pastries, soups and jellies for the evening, as well as luncheon for the Mistress. Sometimes I have a short rest in the afternoon, but if there are guests there is no time for resting – we have to prepare fish, roasts, vegetables and sauces and all must be ready at the right time. After dinner is served and eaten, my day is over – but the kitchen maids and scullery maids must wash up and clean the kitchen before they can go to bed.'

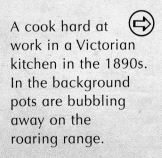

A cook hard at work in a Victorian kitchen in the 1890s. In the background pots are bubbling away on the roaring range.

Victorian households

Victorian families were larger than those of today, with the average family having six children. In well-off families, the father was the head of the household and went out to work, while the mother stayed and looked after the home.

⬆ A young boy cleans shoes to earn a few pennies. This early photograph was taken in 1877.

The working class

In poorer homes, however, it was often necessary for the whole family to work. Many young children were employed in mines, mills and factories, although laws passed in the 1860s and 1870s gradually limited the age and the number of hours that children were allowed to work. Other children worked on the streets, cleaning shoes, sweeping chimneys or selling flowers, firewood, fruit or buttons.

Servants

Working families who could afford it would employ a maid to help with all tasks around the home. Middle class families usually had a few servants, including a cook and a nursemaid. In 1871, there were more than 1 million servants in Britain, and more women were employed in domestic service than any other occupation.

It was a hard life

Many girls were less than 15 years old when they left their homes to work as servants. In return for their food, somewhere to sleep (often in the kitchen) and a small wage, they were expected to work long hours. If they were lucky they might get half a day off on Sunday afternoons – as long as their jobs were finished first.

In middle-class families, the mistress of the house was responsible for supervising her servants. In her *Book of Household Management*, Mrs Beeton advised that every morning the mistress should check that jobs such as cleaning had been done properly, before going to the kitchen to give orders about food for the day, and to unlock the store cupboard to give out the necessary supplies.

⬆ This photograph of a Victorian household was taken in 1885. The female servants are all wearing white aprons.

Mrs Beeton, 1836–1865

Isabella Beeton was born in 1836. In 1856 she married Samuel Beeton, a publisher of books and magazines, and began to write articles on household management and cookery for some of her husband's publications. She is famous for her 'Book of Household Management,' published in 1861. It gives advice on all aspects of running a Victorian household as well as containing a large number of recipes.

Children at home

While the children of poor families often lived and slept in the same room as their parents and brothers and sisters, children in wealthier families spent their early lives in the nursery.

Life in the nursery

The nursery was usually one or two rooms at the top of the house, near to the servants' rooms. Children played and had lessons in the day nursery, and slept in the night nursery. Rich families employed a full-time nanny who took complete charge of the children and babies. The nanny, often known to the children as Nurse, fed and dressed them, played with them, took them for walks, and put them to bed. Most mothers spent some time with their children everyday, and fathers would see them briefly at bedtime.

⇩ A Victorian nanny at work in the nursery.

Struggling to survive

In the 1840s, three out of every 20 children died before the age of one. But in the slums of Liverpool, among some of the very poorest people, half of all children died before reaching their fifth birthday. Poor children in large families were often looked after by older **siblings**, and it was not uncommon for babies to be sent away to live with relatives if their parents could not afford to feed them.

Written at the time

In her novel *East Lynne*, published in 1861, Mrs Henry Wood wrote about the children's place in the home:

'Let the offices, properly belonging to a nurse, be performed by the nurse ... Let her have the trouble of the children, their noise, their romping; in short, let the nursery be her place and the children's place. But I hope I shall never fail to gather my children round me daily, at stated periods, for higher purposes ... This is a mother's task ...'

Toys and pastimes

Wealthy parents could afford to buy toys for their children, such as wax dolls, dolls' houses, rocking horses, miniature tea sets, and mechanical train sets. Children spent much of their time indoors playing board games or reading books such as Lewis Carroll's *Alice's Adventures in Wonderland*, which was a great success when it was published in 1865. However poorer families made their own toys, such as peg dolls or paper windmills.

These are the kinds of toys that wealthy Victorian families could afford.

Timeline

1837	Queen Victoria comes to the throne.
1842	Edwin Chadwick publishes *An Inquiry into the Sanitary Conditions of the Labouring Population of Great Britain*.
1846	The Baths and Wash Houses Act allows parishes to build public bath and wash houses.
1848–1849	The cholera outbreak kills thousands across Britain.
1850	Titus Salt begins work on a model community at Saltaire.
1851	The Great Exhibition is held at Crystal Palace in London.
1853–1854	The cholera outbreak kills more than 10,000 people in London.
1858	The 'Great Stink' affects London.
1858	Joseph Bazalgette begins work on a system of sewers for London.
1861	Mrs Beeton's *Book of Household Management* is published.
1866	The Sanitary Act sets out requirements for sewage disposal and the provision of clean water.
1870	Dr Barnardo opens his first home for destitute boys.
1875	The Public Health Act covers a wide range of subjects including water supply, prevention of pollution of water, removal of sewage, housing standards and prevention and control of diseases.
1876	Dr Bernardo opens his first home for destitute girls.
1878	Cragside becomes the first house in the world to be lit by electricity.
1879	George and Richard Cadbury start work on the Bournville estate in Birmingham.
1879	Joseph Swan demostrates the first practical light bulb.
1879	The first telephone exchange opens in London.
1883	Edison & Swan United Electric Light Company is founded.
1901	Queen Victoria dies.

Glossary

architectural describes the design of a building

British Empire a group of territories and countries which were controlled by Britain

butler usually the head male servant in the household who often hired and fired other servants. He was also in charge of security and matters such as the wines and serving at the table

cesspit a covered pit dug to store sewage

cholera a disease which is picked up from dirty water

colony a territory that is ruled by another, usually more powerful, country

cottage industry a type of industry that relies on people who work in their homes (homeworkers)

footman a servant who admits visitors and sometimes serves at the table

Industrial Revolution the name given to a time when steam-powered machinery was developed to do jobs previously done by hand. The Industrial Revolution took place in Britain during the end of the eighteenth and beginning of the nineteeth centuries

mangle a device with two heavy rollers turned by a handle, designed to wring out water and remove wrinkles from washed laundry

mass-production the manufacture of goods on a large scale at a low cost

manufacturing making something with machines, usually in factories

privy a toilet

raw material a substance such as wood or cotton that is used as the basic material for the manufacture of goods

reign the number of years a King or Queen rules over a country

sewage waste and water

sibling brother or sister

smog a mixture of thick fog and air pollution

suburb an area on the edge of a town or city

tenement a large house or building that is divided into flats

terrace a row of houses that all share their side walls

tram a vehicle that runs on rails set into the road

workhouse a place where the sick and destitute could seek shelter and food in return for work

Index

Resources

A Victorian Childhood: At Home Ruth Thomson, Franklin Watts 2007
Facts About: The Victorians Kay Woodward, Wayland 2007
The Victorians reconstructed Liz Gogerly, Wayland 2005

www.bbc.co.uk/schools/victorians
An excellent website that summarises Victorian life.
www.victorianweb.org
Explore many different topics about the Victorians.